Poem of the Week

Creative Cross-Curricular Poems and Grammar, Too!

Grades 3-5

by Betsy Franco

A Teaching Resource Center Publication

Published by
Teaching Resource Center
P.O. Box 82777
San Diego, CA 92138

Project Editor–Anne Linehan
Edited by Laura Woodard
Design and production by Janis Poe
Illustrations by Linda Starr

Printed in the United States of America
ISBN: 1-56785-048-0

Acknowledgements

For my Bubby Bessie
who liked to pat the back of my hand

Thank you to the following teachers
for their input on this book of poems:

Alice Anne Chandler
Leilani Eng
Debbie Hilleary
Janeen Kent
Nan Knoblauch
Andrea Ruggiero
Stacia Sanchez
Fred Wiener

Thank you, as well, to the children
at El Carmelo School who gave me ideas
for the poems by just being themselves.

Choosing Poems

You're free to use the poems in any order that suits you. Even if you're year-round, you're set. To help you appreciate the versatility of the collection, the poems have been organized in two ways:

1. In the table of contents, the curriculum-related poems come first. The "Other" poems are appropriate for any time.

2. In the chart on page 3, the poems have been organized by grammar and punctuation elements. All the poems in the collection are included.

Table of Contents

Introduction
Teacher Notes. 4

Values
"What Goes Around" 10
Turning Down the Heat 11
*My Best Friend and I (Science) 12
*Sharing a Room (Math) 13
New Kid 14
Birthday Money 15
My Moods. 16
Timothy Jones and His Yo-Yo. 17
*Everyone's Family (Social Studies). 18

Science
*The Package That's Me (Math). 19
Habitats 20
*Dear Thomas Alva Edison (Social Studies) 21
The Predator's Bad Day 22
My Favorite Music 23

Math
Math Poems. 24
a bare foot 25
Babysitting 26
Three People and a Pizza. 27

Social Studies
Once There Were Buffalo. 28
Time Travel 29
Imagine 30
Someday. 31

Other
I run 32
You Never Know Which Seeds Will Grow 33
"Crazy Hair Day". 34
Dog on the Loose 35
If...Then 36
Moonlight. 37
tip...toeing. 38
cat fight. 39
Unusual Habits and Unusual Rhymes. 40
A Pack of Wolves 41
Ramona Street in July 42
You're Invited 43
Haunted House Instructions 44
How I Feel About Jobs. 45
Our Tree House 46
Spider in the Tub 47
The Morning Visitor 48
Sounds Before School 49
Braces. 50
Grammar Rules 51

Blacklines 52

*Poems that are in more than one category indicate the additional categories in parentheses.

Poem of the Week Table of Grammar and Punctuation Elements

Grammar/Punctuation Element	Poems	Grammar/Punctuation Element	Poems
nouns	a bare foot 25	series with commas	Once There Were Buffalo 28
	Sharing a Room 13		Time Travel 29
	The Package That's Me 19		Haunted House Instructions 44
verbs, verb tenses	I run 32	colons	How I Feel About Jobs 45
	You Never Know Which Seeds Will Grow . . . 33		"Crazy Hair Day" 34
adjectives	"Crazy Hair Day" 34		Haunted House Instructions 44
	Dog on the Loose 35	end punctuation	Dog on the Loose 35
adverbs	If...Then 36		Birthday Money 15
interesting nouns, verbs, adjectives, and adverbs	Moonlight 37	complete sentences	Three People and a Pizza 27
			The Package That's Me 19
personal pronouns and possessive pronouns	Habitats 20	compound sentences	Birthday Money 15
	Sharing a Room 13		"Crazy Hair Day" 34
prepositions	Imagine 30		Time Travel 29
prefixes and suffixes	The Predator's Bad Day 22	letter format	Dear Thomas Alva Edison 21
	Timothy Jones and His Yo-Yo 17		You're Invited 43
syllables	tip...toeing 38	synonyms	I run 32
word endings: plurals, verb endings	cat fight 39		Our Tree House 46
	Unusual Habits and Unusual Rhymes 40		Turning Down the Heat 11
compound words	Everyone's Family 18	antonyms	Spider in the Tub 47
collective nouns	A Pack of Wolves 41		My Moods 16
chains/families of words	Braces 50	homonyms	The Morning Visitor 48
capitalization	Ramona Street in July 42	simile and metaphor	New Kid 14
	Someday 31		My Best Friend and I 12
abbreviations	You're Invited 43	onomatopoeia	Sounds Before School 49
apostrophes: contractions, possessives	Haunted House Instructions 44	alliteration	Braces 50
	Ramona Street in July 42	synaesthesia	My Favorite Music 23
quotation marks for dialogue	Babysitting 26	grammar rules	Grammar Rules 51
	New Kid 14	"math grammar"	Math Poems 24
	My Favorite Music 23		
quotation marks for sayings, poems, stories, articles	"What Goes Around" 10		
	"Crazy Hair Day" 34		

Teacher Notes

Use *Poem of the Week* to share the rhythm and cadence of poetry and the joy of poetic language with the students in your class. The topics of the poems were chosen to reflect the world of third to fifth graders, making this book a natural, weekly link to the family. And if you choose, you can use each poem
- as the context for raising awareness of grammar and punctuation
- as a tie-in to math, social studies, and science curricula
- as a springboard for values education
- as inspiration for creativity

Overview

Poetry is a mainstay in the classroom. But it's usually up to you to beg, steal, or borrow the poems you need. It's usually your job to find poetry that's relevant, lively, touching, and thematically appropriate.

Relax. The poems are written. The themes are in place. There's one poem per week, including a special set of curriculum-related poems. There's an extra bonus, too. Since grammar plays an important part in students' writing, each poem highlights a particular grammar rule.

If you choose, you can follow the suggestions that accompany each poem. That way, you can enjoy the poetry with your students, while at the same time introducing, teaching, or reviewing relevant grammar skills. The suggestions will also help you integrate the poems into the curriculum.

Along with the poems and suggestions, we've provided strips for each poem that fit into the Desktop Pocket Chart. With all these tools, groups can enjoy the poems, individual students can learn from and elaborate on the poems, and you can relax and enjoy your teaching.

Versatility Plus

You can choose poems by
   theme
   curriculum area
   week
   grammar focus
   your particular interests

What You've Got

- a poem for every week of the year
- a set of thematic poems for curriculum areas and values education
- suggestions on how to bring out the specific grammar focus of each poem
- suggestions for integrating the poems into the curriculum
- suggestions for making the poems personal and interactive for the students
- poetry strips and an illustration that fit into the Desktop Pocket Chart

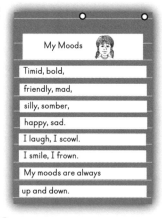

Desktop Pocket Chart
12" wide x 16" high, 10 pockets

Student Poems

For every week of the year, you have a poem, enlarged for easy reading. You can make a copy of the poem for each child, leaving off the Suggestions for Going Further.

Suggestions for Going Further

The suggestions next to the poems are your easy-to-use guides for extending the poems, if the ideas suit your needs. The suggestions point out the grammar elements in the poems and describe how to expand on them. The suggestions also include ideas for using the poems in different areas of your curriculum—science, math, social studies, creative writing, and values education.

F poem strips start on page 60

Suggestions for Going Further

1. The use of quotation marks in the seventh line of the poem brings up the issue of when to use quotation marks and when to underline (or use italics). Have students brainstorm and record examples of both:
• Use quotation marks for the name of a poem, song, or magazine article, and for a saying.
• Underline or italicize the name of a book, magazine, newspaper, ship, movie, or play.
2. Add a blank strip to the end of each line and have students fill it in. Example:
    I helped Bo <u>clean his room.</u>
    Bo helped Mo <u>with his homework.</u>
3. Values: Give students a chance to discuss the saying "What goes around comes around." Can students think of examples from their own lives? (Ask: "Have you ever done someone a favor and had the favor returned? Have you ever taught someone something and learned something yourself?") Explain that the favor or kind action doesn't necessarily "come back around" immediately, or even from the same person you had the interaction with. For example, you might help a neighbor with a chore, and the next week a friend might help you with a chore.
4. Start a bulletin board of quotations, such as
    "The early bird gets the worm."
    "Do unto others as you would have them do unto you."
    "Last but not least."
    "You reap what you sow."
    "Practice makes perfect."
    Encourage students to discuss how the quotations apply to daily life.

5

"What Goes Around"

I helped Bo,
Bo helped Mo,
Mo helped Mei,
Mei helped Ray,
Ray helped Bea,
and Bea helped me.
"What goes around comes around."
That's how it oughta be.

Strips for the Desktop Pocket Chart

You're all set for group work. By copying and cutting out the enlarged strips (starting on page 52) and using them in the Desktop Pocket Chart, you can display a poem for many eyes to see. Groups of children can interact with the poem in this intimate yet practical medium. For sturdier strips, use index tag when copying.

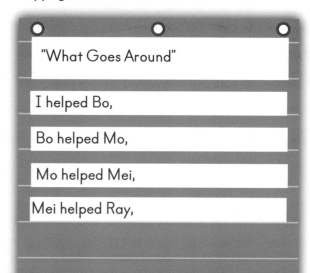

"What Goes Around"

I helped Bo,

Bo helped Mo,

Mo helped Mei,

Mei helped Ray,

Ray helped Bea,

and Bea helped me.

"What goes around comes around."

That's how it oughta be.

There are many ways to use *Poem of the Week.* You can copy the student poems for individual use. You can reconstruct the poem on a Desktop Pocket Chart for group work. You can make your own strips for a standard pocket chart.

Ways to Use the Student Poems

- Read through and select the poem that suits your needs.
- Cut out and adhere the poem to the center of a blank page.
- Add blanks to the poem, if you choose.
- Make a copy of the student poem for each student, with or without Suggestions for Going Further.
- Enjoy the poem for the beauty of the words, the rhythm, and the content.
- Have each student add the poem to a personal poetry anthology.
- Follow the Suggestions for Going Further that make sense to you.
- Send poem books home to be shared with family members.

A knot of toads

Going Further with the Student Poems

→ Make the poems personal and interactive. It's as simple as whiting out or taping over a word or phrase in the student poem before making copies.

> Someday
>
> There were George
> and Thomas and Abe
> and Franklin and John
> and Richard and Bill.
>
> Someday they'll be
> <u>Susan</u> and <u>Degon</u>
> and <u>Marcos</u> and <u>Maria</u>
> and <u>Muhammad</u> and <u>Ruth</u>
> and <u>Meimei</u>.
>
> Someday.

→ Make the poems into word problems.

← Let students illustrate the poem or make an appropriate border for it. This student work illustrates a line from the poem "A Pack of Wolves."

> Babysitting
>
> "Three-fifty an hour," said nice Mrs. Fine.
> "Can you come by tomorrow from 5 to 9?"
> "I'll just ask my mother," I said with a wave.
> "Of course," said my mom. "They're so well-behaved."
>
> I thought to myself, "Well, I like to play games,
> but after four hours, it's not quite the same.
> But I like both her kids and they love me to read.
> Three-fifty times four is just what I need!"
>
> $3.50
> $\underline{\times\ 4}$
> $14.00

How I Feel About Jobs

The jobs I don't like
are listed below:
<u>lion taming</u>, <u>snow-shoveling</u>,
and <u>window-washing</u>.
The jobs I would like
are listed here, too:
<u>ice-cream store owner</u>, <u>baseball
player</u>, and <u>movie star</u>.
So that's how I feel.
Now how about you?

← Let students answer
   questions posed in
   the poems.

↓ White out or tape over punctuation in the poem and let
   students fill it in.

→ Add new verses or write
   variations on the poem.

↓ Have students highlight
   or underline the particular grammar element fea-
   tured in the poem. The
   adverbs have been
   underlined below.

me + brain = smarter

cold + hot = warm

*family
+ new baby
happy*

jacket — sleeves = vest

shells x time = sand

cat + food = fat cat

"Crazy Hair Day"

 It was "Crazy Hair Day"
 and this is what we wore
 silly pigtails in front
 green and blue hair dye
 hair sticking out all over
 and spiked and moussed bangs
 Hey, even the guinea pig
 had his hair sticking every-which-way
 but then he's always having
 a crazy hair day

If...Then

If I cut my toenails,
then the bus won't <u>ever</u> come on time.

If the sun forgets to come up this morning,
then my dog will <u>definitely</u> have fleas.

If my bike has a <u>completely</u> flat tire,
then it won't storm on my birthday.

If my cat washes himself <u>very carefully</u>,
then my dad will take me to miniature golf.

If I make this <u>totally</u> impossible hook shot,
then you have to clean my room for me!

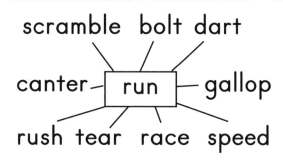

← Make lists or webs of words
   that share a grammar or poetic
   element that is emphasized in
   the poem.

7

Ways to Use the Desktop Pocket Chart

- Copy the poem strips and the illustration onto index tag.
- Cut out the strips and the illustration.
- Reconstruct the poem in the Desktop Pocket Chart. We've numbered each line to minimize confusion. You can keep the numbers or cut them off.
- Gather a group of students and ask for volunteers to read the poem aloud.
- Work with the poem's grammar skill.

Going Further with the Desktop Pocket Chart

- Use nonpermanent markers, Wikki Stix, or highlighting tape to highlight grammar elements on the pocket chart strips. The antonyms have been underlined in the poem below:

- Use sticky notes to cover words in the poem. Let students suggest new words to write in their place to personalize or change the poem. Alternatively, you can use blank word cards made from heavy paper to cover and replace the words. (Cards should be about 2" long, 1" high.)

- Cover phrases in the poem with sticky notes or blank strips and let students interact with the poem by rewriting the phrases. (Strips should be about 1" high.) Below, the poem "Moonlight", page 37, has been rewritten:

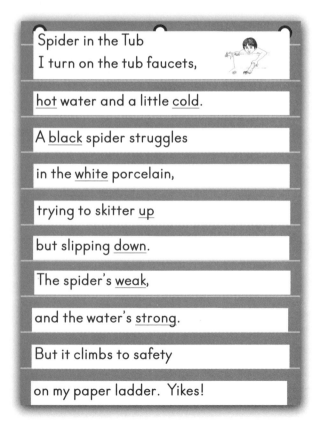

Spider in the Tub
I turn on the tub faucets,

<u>hot</u> water and a little <u>cold</u>.

A <u>black</u> spider struggles

in the <u>white</u> porcelain,

trying to skitter <u>up</u>

but slipping <u>down</u>.

The spider's <u>weak</u>,

and the water's <u>strong</u>.

But it climbs to safety

on my paper ladder. Yikes!

Sharing a Room

Sally Sue is very messy,

She leaves *clothes* thrown everywhere.

She's got *rotten food* on her bookshelf,

spilled soda on her chair.

A Spaceship

A spaceship

golden and menacing

zoomed boldly

over to the window...

↓ Use chart paper to create banks or webs of words with the same grammatical or poetic elements as the poem.

→ Cut the poem strips into individual words. Have students use the words from the poem to make new poetic sentences.

Habitats

The lizard slithers out of bed.

The frog covers the bedroom floor.

The bat and lizard crawl under the rocks.

I clean my shirt on the edge of the sun.

I folded my warm frog in my wings.

He makes her toss up his morning meal.

He sets his bat on the moon.

prefixes

predator

predicament

consumption

connection

conclusion

disappears

understands

suffixes

motion

connection

conclusion

consumption

predicament

sensational

↓ Cut a word from one of the poem strips into individual letters. See how many words the students can make using only these letters.

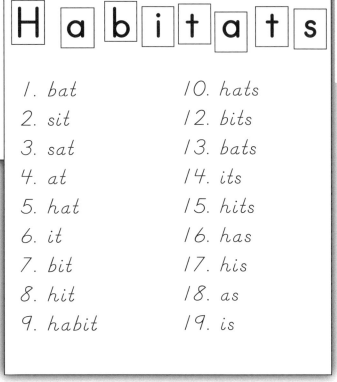

Habitats

1. *bat*
2. *sit*
3. *sat*
4. *at*
5. *hat*
6. *it*
7. *bit*
8. *hit*
9. *habit*

10. *hats*
12. *bits*
13. *bats*
14. *its*
15. *hits*
16. *has*
17. *his*
18. *as*
19. *is*

Suggestions for Going Further

1. The use of quotation marks in the seventh line of the poem brings up the issue of when to use quotation marks and when to underline (or use italics). Have students brainstorm and record examples of both:
   • Use quotation marks for the title of a poem, song, or magazine article, and for a saying.
   • Underline or italicize the name of a book, magazine, newspaper, ship, movie, or play.
2. Add a blank strip to the end of each line and have students fill it in. Example:
   > I helped Bo <u>clean his room.</u>
   > Bo helped Mo <u>with his homework.</u>
3. Values: Give students a chance to discuss the saying "What goes around comes around." Can students think of examples from their own lives? (Ask: "Have you ever done someone a favor and had the favor returned? Have you ever taught someone something and learned something yourself?") Explain that the favor or kind action doesn't necessarily "come back around" immediately, or even from the same person you had the interaction with. For example, you might help a neighbor with a chore, and the next week a friend might help you with a chore.
4. Start a bulletin board of quotations, such as
   "The early bird gets the worm."
   "Do unto others as you would have them do unto you."
   "Last but not least."
   "You reap what you sow."
   "Practice makes perfect."
   Encourage students to discuss how the quotations apply to daily life.

"What Goes Around"

I helped Bo,
Bo helped Mo,
Mo helped Mei,
Mei helped Ray,
Ray helped Bea,
and Bea helped me.
"What goes around comes around."
That's how it oughta be.

poem strips start on page 54

Suggestions for Going Further

1. There are a number of synonyms for *angry* in this poem. Make a web with the word *angry* in the middle and the other words from the poem around it. Let students add to the web. Some possibilities include *mad, fuming, raging, storming, burning, blazing,* and *irate.* Students can use a thesaurus when they run out of ideas.
2. Start another web with synonyms for *calm*. Possibilities include *cool, mellow, peaceful, mellow, quiet, restful, at ease, composed, relaxed,* and *serene.*
3. Values: Discuss the situation posed by the poem. What has this person done to calm down from something that made him very angry? Ask students to brainstorm things they could do when they feel themselves heating up with anger. Possibilities include the following:
   take deep breaths
   walk away
   count to ten
   write about it
   beat on a pillow or inanimate object
Ask students what they could do after calming down. Some may suggest going back to the person they were angry at and talking about the situation.

Turning Down the Heat

Ticked off

Angry

Furious

Boiling

That was how my feelings grew.

Breathing

deeply

Cooling

down

Now that has changed my point of view!

poem strips start on page 55

Suggestions for Going Further

1. By using *metaphor* (a comparison of two different things without the word *like*), this poem compares friendship to the relationship between two magnets. Have students decide if this is a good comparison and if it holds true for their friendships.
2. Science:
   • Have students use magnets to duplicate the images in the poem.
   • Let them search for objects in the room that are magnetic. (Remind them to keep magnets away from computers.)
   • Have students explore the force of a magnet, and how strongly it attracts and repels.
   • Ask students to compare the strength of different magnets.
3. Values: Friendships have a way of going up and down, as the poem describes. Give students a chance to write about times their friendships have been challenged and how they solved, or didn't solve, the problem(s) that came up. It's important to know that even strong relationships can fluctuate and that it takes work to maintain them.

My Best Friend and I

Sometimes we're magnets,
drawn to each other like
a negative and a positive force.
Other days we're like two positives
(or more like two negatives)
pushing away from each other,
never able to get too close.
But then we flip around somehow
and we're inseparable again.

poem strips start on page 57

Suggestions for Going Further

1. Use this poem to explore nouns. Have students highlight or underline all the nouns on their copies of the poem. Remind them that a noun is a person, place, or thing. The only confusing noun in the poem is the word *more* in the third verse.
2. Encourage students to find all the pronouns (*she, me, I, you, we, it*) and possessive pronouns (*her, my*). These can be underlined in a different color than the nouns.
3. On the Desktop Pocket Chart, white out the words *toys, laundry,* and *gobs of toothpaste*. Have students write a new version of the verse by filling in the blanks.
4. Math: Give students grid paper and explain that the room in the poem is represented by sixteen squares (4x4). Let them find at least six ways to divide the room in half. Possibilities include the following:

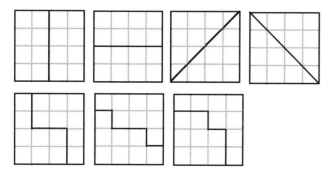

4. Values: Talk about how the two very different siblings in this poem negotiate (talk about things to reach an agreement) and compromise to solve their problems.

13

Sharing a Room

Sally Sue is very messy.
She leaves toys thrown everywhere.
She's got laundry on her bookshelf,
gobs of toothpaste on her chair.

As for me, I'm neat and tidy.
I have labels on each drawer.
Everyday I use the vacuum.
You could eat right off my floor.

We divided up the bedroom,
drew a line across the floor.
We made sure that it was even,
neither one was getting more.

She allows me in the closet,
and I let her use the door.
Though the plan is not quite perfect,
it's much better than before!

from *Counting Caterpillars and Other Math Poems* (Scholastic, 1998)
Note: You can display two verses at a time.

poem strips start on page 59

Suggestions for Going Further

1. A *simile* is a comparison of two different things, using the word *like*. Ask students to explain the two similes in the poem and tell why they help express the ideas in the poem. For example, a scarecrow looks awkward, and rather than making friends, it scares off visitors. A yo-yo goes up and down, and this child is moving in and out of the crowd of children as she becomes brave and then shy about trying to make friends.
2. Values: Have students discuss some of the pluses and minuses of being a new kid. Brainstorm different ways in which a new kid can be made to feel welcome in the classroom and on the playground.
3. Let students analyze the punctuation in the direct quote at the end of the poem. Then have them think of other friendly things Joe might say, such as:
   "Wanna stick around?"
   "Wait up."
   "Come and play with us."
   "Come on over."
   "Hello" or "Hi."
   "Hey, Sam!"

New Kid

Like a scarecrow,
I stand with awkward arms,
while everyone laughs and plays.
Like a yo-yo,
I move in and out
of the crowd of kids.
I guess I'll go home alone again.
But hey!
There's Joe and he's yelling,
"Wanna play?"

Suggestions for Going Further

1. The first verse of the poem provides a nice springboard for discussing when a sentence is compound or not. Point out that the first sentence requires a comma before the word *and* because it is compound. Have students underline the subject and verb in each part of the compound sentence.

   <u>My auntie gave</u> me birthday cash,
   and <u>I'm wondering</u> what to do.

   The second sentence is not a compound sentence because the phrase after the word *and* could not stand alone; it has no subject. Have students underline the subject and the verbs in this sentence.

   <u>I might</u> see movies all day long
   and <u>bring</u> a friend or two.

2. Values: The value highlighted in this poem is responsibility. Let students describe how the person in the poem is taking responsibility. Students may have stories about taking responsibility that they could share with the class or write about in their journals.

Birthday Money

My auntie gave me birthday cash,
and I'm wondering what to do.
I might see movies all day long
and bring a friend or two.

Oh no, I just remembered
what I really need to do.
I have to pay for the window
that my soccer ball went through!

This is a variation on the poem "Birthday Money" published in *Counting Caterpillars and Other Math Poems* (Scholastic, 1998)

poem strips start on page 62

Suggestions for Going Further

1. *Antonyms* (words that have opposite meanings) are the basis of this poem. Have students find and record all the antonym pairs—some are adjectives and some are verbs. Then brainstorm additions to the list. Try to add some adverbs such as *happily* and *merrily*.
2. Let students choose a pair of antonyms and illustrate them using pictures cut from magazines.
3. Values: It's important for people to recognize, and take responsibility for, their feelings. Otherwise, people have a tendency to blame and take out their feelings on others. Have students write journal entries about situations that have put them in different moods.

My Moods

Timid, bold,

friendly, mad,

silly, somber,

happy, sad.

I laugh, I scowl.

I smile, I frown.

My moods are always

up and down.

Suggestions for Going Further

1. Use this poem as a springboard for talking about prefixes. Display the poem in the Desktop Pocket Chart and have students find and highlight the prefixes:
   beginning   unwind   untangle   unbelievable
2. Let students brainstorm other words with prefixes:

be-	un-	dis-	bi-
beside	unfit	dislike	biceps
before	unfold	disturb	bicycle
befriend	unable	disbelief	bisect
beneath	unpleasant	display	binoculars
belong	uncover	disrupt	
below	ungrateful	disappear	
became			

3. Values: Talk about the value of passing on a skill or teaching someone how to do something. It contributes to the community, strengthens friendships, and gives the teacher and the student confidence. Let students talk about skills that they could teach or have taught someone else. They can also discuss skills others have taught them. You might want to set aside time for students to teach a skill they know to the class.

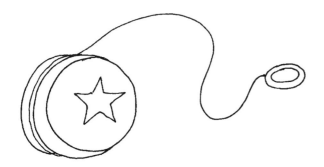

17

Timothy Jones and His Yo-Yo

In the beginning,
I couldn't do much—
just make it unwind
and untangle the string.
Then Timothy taught me 'bout
walkin' the dog, hoppin' the fence,
and a lot of cool things.
It's quite unbelievable, let me tell you,
what Timothy Jones and his yo-yo can do.

poem strips start on page 64

Suggestions for Going Further

1. Have students find all the compound words in the poem: *everyone's, someplace, peacetime, wartime, pigtails, upset.* Keep a running list of compound words in the classroom.
2. Social Studies: Put up a map of the world on a bulletin board, and let students put pushpins in the parts of the world from which their families originated. They could even pin a piece of yarn from the map to a picture of themselves. Help students realize that everyone but American Indians came from somewhere else and yet we're all Americans. You might want to read some books on immigration, such as *Molly's Pilgrim* by Barbara Cohen (Lothrop, Lee & Shepard, 1983) or *I Hate English* by Ellen Levine (Scholastic, 1989).
3. Values: Respect for all cultures is very important in today's world. Have students ask their parents and grandparents about traditions or objects that the family has kept from the "homeland." These could be simple songs, recipes, holiday traditions, keepsakes, and so on. Give each student a chance to share with the class.

18

Everyone's Family

Everyone's family's from someplace else
(except for American Indians).
Families came from close and far,
in peacetime and in wartime, too.
Some wore babushkas on their heads,
and some had pigtails down their backs.
Some felt upset, but most had hope
for their life in America—different and new.

Note: A *babushka* is a head scarf, pronounced "buh-boosh-kah".

Suggestions for Going Further

1. Have students find all the interesting adjectives in the poem and underline them. Then underline them on the strips in the Desktop Pocket Chart using highlighter tape or markers. The adjectives include *snow-white, sinewy, pulsating, protective.*

2. Science: Have students describe other things that are included in the "package". These might include the brain, lungs, stomach, intestines, liver, bladder, kidneys, pancreas, eyes or glands. Students can add new verses to the poem by describing these additional organs using intriguing adjectives.

3. Math: Have students map out 20 square feet outdoors. Have them use the atlas or almanac to find distances that are 60,000 miles long. How many times would that be back and forth across the United States, or up and down the Mississippi River? Present other word problems based on the poem: If there are 25 bones in the spine, 27 bones in each hand, and 26 bones in each foot, how many bones are in the rest of the body? (75) About what fraction of the 206 bones are in the hands and feet? (about ½)

The Package That's Me

206 snow-white

bones covered by more than

600 sinewy muscles nourished by

60,000 miles of pulsating blood

vessels and encased in

20 square feet of protective

skin which also houses

a heart the size of a fist

that brings it all to life.

poem strips start on page 67

Suggestions for Going Further

1. Let students hunt for all the personal pronouns and possessive pronouns in the poem, along with the animals or people they refer to. Students can underline or highlight the pronouns on the Desktop Pocket Chart version of the poem (*she, he, I , her, his, my*). They can also use blank word cards to change the gender of the animals, along with the related pronouns.

2. Science:
   - Discuss the definition of *habitat*—the place an animal naturally chooses to live because that place has the conditions it needs to survive, such as food, water, shelter, weather, elevation, and space.
   - Have students identify the habitats in the poem.
   - Let students brainstorm and research the habitats of other wild animals such as the ones below:

Animal	Habitat
fiddler crab	beaches
land snails	woodlands or gardens
giraffe	grasslands
white-tailed deer	temperate forests
spider monkey	tropical rainforest
gila monster	desert
penguins	Antarctica

3. Students can describe and draw their own habitats at home. Have them include these features: food, water, shelter, weather, and space.

20

Habitats

The lizard slithers from under the rocks.

She warms her scales in the morning sun.

The frog sets up camp on the edge of the pond.

He contemplates his afternoon meal.

The bat unfurls his folded wings.

He exits his cave to hunt by the moon.

I throw off the covers and crawl out of bed.

I toss a shirt on my bedroom floor.

But unlike the lizard, the frog, and the bat,

my mom makes me clean up my habitat!

poem strips start on page 68

Suggestions for Going Further

1. Review the parts of a letter: date, greeting, main body of text, salutation, and signature.
2. Science: Talk about Edison's inventions. Then brainstorm other inventors and inventions, discoverers and discoveries. Take books out of the library for students to study. Then let students pick an inventor, research her or him, and write a letter. Some possibilities:

   Sumerians: writing (around 3500 B.C.)
   Archimedes: mathematical discoveries (in the 200s B.C.)
   Cai Lun: paper (105 A.D.)
   Maya civilization: accurate yearly calendar (around 250 A.D.)
   Bi Sheng (Pi Sheng): movable type for printing (1045 A.D.)
   Lady Mary Montagu: smallpox vaccination (around 1717) (credited to Edward Jenner)
   Louis Braille: Braille (1824)
   Alexander Graham Bell: telephone (1875)
   Marie E. Allen: diaper (1887)
   George Washington Carver: more than 300 uses for the peanut (around 1896) (African American)
   Marie Curie: research on radioactivity (1898)
   Isadora Duncan: free expression in dance (around 1899)
   Wright Brothers: first successful airplane flight on record (1903)
   Chien Chiung Wu: experiments with atomic parity (1956) (woman)
   Richard B. Spikes: automatic safety brakes (1962) (African American)
   Martine Kempf: voice-controlled wheelchair (1982)
   Lonnie Johnson: Super Soaker squirt gun (1982) (African American)

June 4, 2000

Dear Thomas Alva Edison,
   Someone invented the Internet
and someone invented the wheel.
But you're the greatest inventor,
at least that's the way I feel.
You made the electric lightbulb,
the movie camera, the phonograph.
If I'd been alive when you were alive,
I would have asked for your autograph.
Sincerely,
Jamie Taft

poem strips start on page 70

Suggestions for Going Further

1. Have students underline the prefixes and suffixes in the poem using different colors to distinguish one prefix or suffix from another. Make a chart of the results:

pre-	-tion/-sion	con-	misc.
predator	motion	connection	predicament
predicament	connection	consumption	sensational
	consumption	conclusion	understands
	conclusion		disappears

2. Let students add to the chart above and brainstorm words with other prefixes and suffixes as well. Examples:
   pre: prediction preprinted preview prevent
   tion/sion: tension mention selection prevention
   con: condition contraction contract
   al: accidental rental experimental
   under: understand underestimate underline
   dis: disappoint dislike dismiss display
   ment/sent: compliment experiment present represent
   re: redo replay repaint reread
   able: desirable valuable portable disabled comfortable
   Note: A rhyming dictionary can be helpful in the case of suffixes, a dictionary in the case of prefixes.
3. Have students make a chart of predators and their prey. Some possibilities: spider and fly, lion and zebra, duck and snail.

For poetry exercises using prefixes and suffixes, see *The Secret Life of Words* by Betsy Franco and Maria Damon (Teaching Resource Center, 2000).

The Predator's Bad Day

The predator
spots its prey,
who understands
its predicament,
snaps into motion,
and disappears.
There is no connection.
There is no consumption—
a sad conclusion for the predator,
but a sensational day for the prey!

poem strips start on page 71

Suggestions for Going Further

1. This poem introduces *simile* and *synaesthesia*. Have students find the simile, which is a comparison between two different things using the word *like*. (*My music sounds like the roof...*) Then explain synaesthesia, which is using one of the five senses to describe something, but using that sense in a way that it is not normally used. For example, music is not really a color and doesn't have a taste. Have students work as a class, in partners, or as individuals to describe their favorite music.

2. Let students highlight the quotation marks in Mom's response.

3. Science: Discuss and experiment with the science of sound.
   - Students can strum a rubber band stretched between their fingers to feel the *vibrations* they are making.
   - Talk about the *frequency*, or the vibrations per second. Have pairs of students stretch and strum a rubber band to decide if the vibrations per second are faster for low or high sounds. (*Sound waves* are closer together and slower for low sounds.) Talk about the limited range of human hearing in the upper frequencies.
   - Have students guess the *decibels* (the intensity or loudness) of these common sounds: whispering (20 dB), normal talking (60 dB), telephone ringing (70 dB), vacuum cleaner (80 dB), air drills (100 dB), amplified rock band (120 dB), jet taking off nearby (140 dB). Explain that sounds that are 140 decibels or more cause pain to humans.

My Favorite Music

My music sounds
like the roof is being torn off.
It's blacks and reds and shocking pinks,
and it tastes like burning rubber.
"The decibels!
The frequencies!
The vibrations!
My eardrums!"
yells Mom.
"Turn *that music* down!!"

Suggestions for Going Further

1. Talk about "math grammar." Math grammar could include the symbols you use, such as +, −, x, ÷, = and $\overline{)}$. Math grammar could also include how you line up addition, subtraction, multiplication, and division problems (with the *ones* under the *ones*, the *tens* under the *tens*, and so on.)
2. Suggest that the students write some "math Poems" of their own. Possible topics include one of the seasons, animal behavior, and everyday activities or events at home or at school.

For activities about mathematical poetry, see *The Secret Life of Words* by Betsy Franco and Maria Damon (Teaching Resource Center, 2000).

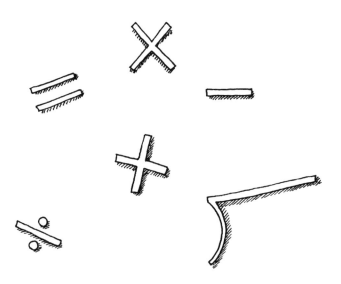

Math Poems*

$$\text{wind } \overline{)\frac{\text{colors}}{\text{fall}}}$$
-leaves
winter

thunder
lightning
wind
<u>+ rain that's warm</u>
summer storm

child
<u>- nap</u>
whining

squirrels in winter
<u>x 3 months</u>
hibernation

* adapted from a poetry form introduced by the poet Bob Grumann

poem strips start on page 74

Suggestions for Going Further

1. Math: Challenge students to find all the nouns in the poem. Note that *time* is a noun in this instance. Then ask the students, "About what fraction of the poem is nouns?" (9/19 or about 1/2)
2. The poem feels like it rhymes, even though the rhyme scheme is not formal, or obvious. The reason for this is the off-rhymes (almost-rhymes), the alliteration (use of the same sound and/or letter), and the repetition. Have students find these three elements in the poem:

Off-Rhymes:	Alliteration:	Repetition:
yelp - welt	a <u>b</u>are foot	<u>some</u> ache
ice - time	a <u>b</u>um<u>b</u>lebee	<u>some</u> ice
		<u>some</u> shoes

For poetry activities involving nouns and off-rhymes, see *The Secret Life of Words* by Betsy Franco and Maria Damon (Teaching Resource Center, 2000).

a bare foot

a bumblebee

a sting

a yelp

a welt

some ache

some ice

some shoes

next time!

Suggestions for Going Further

1. This entire poem is a conversation! Have students highlight every punctuation mark in the poem.
2. Then have them rewrite the poem. (Their versions don't have to rhyme.) Perhaps Mrs. Fine isn't offering very much money. Perhaps the narrator's mother disapproves or the kids are wild.
3. Math:
   - Have students figure out how much the narrator will be paid. ($3.50 x 4 = $14.00)
   - What if Mrs. Fine and her husband call to say they will be two hours late? Then how much will the babysitter receive? ($3.50 x 6 = $21.00)
   - Have students figure out the total pay in the versions of the poems they wrote.
   - Let students talk about jobs they have had, how much they were paid per hour, and how much they were paid in all.

Babysitting

"Three-fifty an hour," said nice Mrs. Fine.
"Can you come by tomorrow from 5 to 9?"
"I'll just ask my mother," I said with a wave.
"Of course," said my mom. "They're so well-behaved."

I thought to myself, "Well, I like to play games,
but after four hours, it's not quite the same.
But I like both her kids and they love me to read.
Three-fifty times four is just what I need!"

Suggestions for Going Further

1. This poem is written in complete sentences. Have students use two different colors to mark the subjects and verbs in each sentence. This can be done on the student poems and/or on the Desktop Pocket Chart.
2. Math: The poem describes a pizza that has been cut into fourths and must be divided equally among 3 people. Have students show how this could be done.
   Solution: If you divide each of the fourths into thirds, then you have twelve twelfths. Each person could eat $\frac{4}{12}$ or $\frac{1}{3}$ of the pizza.

$\frac{4}{12} + \frac{4}{12} + \frac{4}{12} + \frac{4}{12} = 3 \times \frac{4}{12} = \frac{12}{12} = 1$ whole pizza

27

Three People and a Pizza

The pepperoni pizza had been
cut up into fourths.
We couldn't divide it evenly,
as you can see, of course.

Then Julie cut each piece again.
She cut them into thirds.
At first her cutting seemed to make
the problem even worse.

But then she passed the pieces out—
to me and her and Steven.
Why sure enough, it all worked out,
and all our shares were even!

Note: Put the first two verses in the Desktop Pocket Chart. Have students solve the math problem in suggestion 2. Then display the third verse.

poem strips start on page 78

Suggestions for Going Further

1. Every sentence in this poem contains a list with commas and a conjunction (*and*). Let students identify each list and generalize about how a list is punctuated.
2. Challenge students to make a list of their own. Possibilities are
   all the uses of a piece of string
   all the ways to cook and use a potato
   Encourage them to be playful and imaginative.
3. Social Studies: The history of the buffalo population reflects the treatment of Indians in early America. Explain to students that in 1890, there were about 30 million buffalo, and the Plains Indians worshipped and depended on the buffalo for their way of life. By 1890 there were less than 1,000 buffalo, and today there are about 200,000 on ranches and preserves. Have students use encyclopedias or other reference sources to find out how lives of American Indians changed after the arrival of Europeans. Let students report on different aspects of that history.

Once There Were Buffalo

They used the buffalo for food,
leather clothing, tipis, robes,
blankets, spoons, cups, knives,
bowstrings, and musical instruments.
Then along came the railroad,
sharpshooters like Wild Bill Cody, and more.
And after a while, there weren't
many buffalo for musical instruments,
bowstrings, knives, cups, spoons, blankets,
robes, tipis, leather clothing, or food.

poem strips start on page 80

Suggestions for Going Further

1. The conjunction *but* is used in the last sentence of the poem. Let it be a springboard for talking about conjunctions (*and, but, or,* etc.) and how to punctuate sentences that include them. Have students notice the comma before *but.* Explain that the two clauses separated by the conjunction can each stand alone.
2. This poem also has two sets of lists. The lists are separated by commas and include the conjunction *and.* Have students find these and note the punctuation. Let students write a list of their favorite foods.
3. Social Studies: Talk about the unusual dishes served in colonial times and solicit students' reactions to them.
4. Social Studies: Brainstorm interesting times in history. Have students decide what period of time they'd like to visit in a time machine. Let them write about the reasons for their choices. Have students exchange papers with partners and check each other's papers for correct punctuation.

29

Time Travel

I thought it would be fun
to come over on the Mayflower,
until I heard that the colonists ate
sheep's tongue pie, stewed eel,
creamed turkey and oysters,
and boiled pigeons.
Peanut chews, hot molasses cider,
and apple pie sound good, but
I think I'll pass on the Mayflower
for now.

Suggestions for Going Further

1. The prepositional phrases used in the poem are used as adverbs. Let students highlight the prepositional phrases on the Desktop Pocket Chart and tell you whether they describe *how, why, where,* or *when.*

in a covered wagon	on a wagon bed
for the night fire	along steep mountain passes
in your nighttime blanket	across rivers
on those covered wagons	

2. Social Studies: Bring in some library books about the covered wagon days. Let students add lines to the poem using interesting facts they find.
3. Social Studies: Let students pick any time in history that you have studied this year, and have them write an "Imagine" poem of their own.

Imagine

Can you imagine being in a covered wagon
and picking up buffalo chips for the night fire?
Can you imagine snakes and spiders
nestled in your nighttime blanket?
What must it be like to float across rivers
on a wagon bed
or wobble along steep mountain passes?
Someone like you was on those covered wagons.
Imagine.

Suggestions for Going Further

1. Social Studies:
   - Ask students to explain what this poem is about. Do they recognize the names of the presidents of the United States in the first verse? What do they know about these presidents in terms of race and gender? Discuss current campaigns and elections. Have any changes been made?
   - Place blank word cards over the names in the second verse on the Desktop Pocket Chart. Let students substitute names for the ones in the poem.
   - For a long-term project, older students can use newspapers to look for potential female and minority candidates for President.
2. All the names in the poem are capitalized. Have children brainstorm a list of other types of words that are capitalized: holidays (*Memorial Day*), buildings (*Empire State Building*), months (*January*), languages (*English, Spanish*), places (*Cleveland, Texas, Africa*), companies and organizations (*Girl Scouts of America*), and planets (*Mars*).

Someday

There were George and Thomas and Abe and Franklin and John and Richard and Bill.

Someday they'll be Barbara and Ebony and Sarah and Tolu and Shoko and Aziz and José.

Someday.

poem strips are on page 84

Suggestions for Going Further

1. Let students find all the verbs in the poem and group them into families according to their meanings. (Note that there are many related words.)

        run - race
        leap - lunge - dive
        catch - squeeze - capture

2. In pairs, have students make webs of synonyms (and related words) for the word *run*. Encourage them to use interesting verbs. Combine ideas into a large class web.

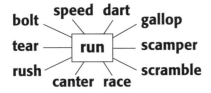

3. Have students rewrite the poem and change the context or the outcome. Perhaps the child drops the ball. Perhaps he's not playing baseball at all—maybe he's trying to catch something that slipped out of his hands.

For poetry activities involving verbs, see *The Secret Life of Words* by Betsy Franco and Maria Damon (Teaching Resource Center, 2000).

I run

I race

I leap

I lunge

I dive

I catch

I squeeze

I capture the ball

at the tip of my mitt.

What a feeling I get!

Suggestions for Going Further

1. Students can explore and identify the verb tenses in each verse of the poem (past, present, and future tense).
2. Then explain that *irregular verbs* do not follow the usual patterns of conjugation in the present tense, past tense and/or past participle. Introduce the irregular verbs below, and have students think of others.

present	past	past participle (past with *have* or *has*)
swim	swam	swum
buy	bought	bought
tell	told	told
rise	rose	risen
lay	laid	laid
fly	flew	flown

3. Ask students to think about their present activities and interests. Have them write about any "seeds" that might grow into future careers for them. Or if they have a dream career, have them write about things they could do in the present to reach their goal.

33

You Never Know Which Seeds Will Grow

When Bo was very little,
he had lots and lots of pets.
Right now he cares for neighbors' dogs.
Someday he'll be a vet.

Kathleen made hook shots in the sink
a long, long time ago.
Right now she is a point guard,
and someday she'll be a pro.

You never know
which seeds will grow!

Extra verse:

Samantha used to put on skits
and sing with her guitar.
Right now she has the lead in plays.
Someday she'll be a star.

Suggestions for Going Further

1. This poem has a number of grammatical elements that students can find. For example, it includes a list with a colon before it. Have students decide if the list in this poem is a list of nouns, verbs, adjectives, or adverbs (nouns). Before copying the student poem, you might want to white out some or all of the punctuation so students can fill it in.
2. Let students also find the compound sentence with the conjunction *but*, which is the last sentence of the poem. Have students find the two parts of the compound sentence, and point out that each could stand alone. Create compound sentence frames and let students complete them.

   I would _____, and I would look _____ if we had a "Crazy Hair Day."
3. The phrase "Crazy Hair Day" is in quotes. Let students think of other elements that are placed inside quotation marks, such as titles of songs, poems, and magazine articles.
4. Have a "Crazy Hair Day" of your own, and let students write about it.

"Crazy Hair Day"

It was "Crazy Hair Day,"
and this is what we wore:
silly pigtails in front,
green and blue hair dye,
hair sticking out all over,
and spiked and moussed bangs.
Hey, even the guinea pig
had his hair sticking every-which-way,
but then he's always having
a crazy hair day!

poem strips start on page 89

Suggestions for Going Further

1. *Adjectives* (describing words) are the focus in this poem about a dog who has gotten loose. Have students highlight the adjectives on their student poems.

    yippy, yappy
    black
    white
    old, mangled
    drippy, slobbery
    softly-padded

2. Display the poem in the Desktop Pocket Chart and cover the adjectives with sticky notes or blank word cards. Let students rewrite the poem using different descriptive words.

3. Let students find all the end punctuation in the poem (periods, question mark, exclamation point). Then have a volunteer read the poem out loud, emphasizing the end punctuation.

4. Challenge students to write a flyer describing a dog or cat that is missing. What information has to appear? What information will help someone identify the animal? What information will make people want to help find the missing pet? Encourage them to use plenty of adjectives in their descriptions.

Dog on the Loose

He's yippy and yappy
with a deep black coat and bold white spots.
Bring out an old, mangled tennis ball,
and he'll be all over you.
He'll shake with his softly-padded paw
if you only ask.
But watch out for his drippy, slobbery tongue.
Have you seen him?
That dog is loose again!
Oh yes, his name is *Houdini.*

poem strips start on page 90

Suggestions for Going Further

1. An *adverb* spruces up each pair of lines. Remind students that adverbs tell *how, where,* and *when* and that they can describe verbs, adjectives, and other adverbs. Let students search for the adverbs and mark them on their student poems. (*ever, definitely, completely, very carefully, totally*) On the Desktop Pocket Chart, have students use blank word cards to replace some of the adverbs in the poem with new ones.
2. Let students make up their own whimsical "If...then" statements. Have each student make four "If...then" sentences that make sense. Next have them cut them apart and mix up the "then..." portions of the sentences. Finally, have them glue down the new sentences and share them with the class.

For whole class poetry exercises using "If...then" dependent clauses, see *The Secret Life of Words* by Betsy Franco and Maria Damon (Teaching Resource Center, 2000).

If...Then

If I cut my toenails,
then the bus won't ever come on time.

If the sun forgets to come up this morning,
then my dog will definitely have fleas.

If my bike has a completely flat tire,
then it won't storm on my birthday.

If my cat washes himself very carefully,
then my dad will take me to miniature golf.

If I make this totally impossible hook shot,
then you'll have to clean my room for me!

poem strips start on page 91

Suggestions for Going Further

1. There are many interesting nouns, verbs, adjectives, and adverbs in this poem. Let students find ones they feel are interesting and sort them according to parts of speech:

nouns	verbs	adjectives	adverbs
moonlight	tiptoed	fragile	mindlessly
glow	burst	fleeting	
	rousing	luminous	
		Technicolor	

2. Discuss how the moonlight is spoken about as if it were a person. Identify this technique as *personification*, and let students find the lines in which moonlight is treated as if it were alive.
3. Have students write about an animal's dream using intriguing nouns, verbs, adjectives, and adverbs.
4. On the Desktop Pocket Chart, let students insert different words for *moonlight* (e.g., *sunlight, firelight, a sunbeam, starlight, a spaceship*), *fragile and fleeting*, and *mindlessly tiptoed*.

> **Example:**
> A spaceship
> golden and menacing
> zoomed boldly
> over to the window...

For poetry exercises using interesting nouns, verbs, adjectives, and adverbs, see *The Secret Life of Words* by Betsy Franco and Maria Damon (Teaching Resource Center, 2000).

Moonlight

Moonlight
fragile and fleeting
tiptoed mindlessly
over to the window
and burst through,
filling the room with
a luminous glow
and rousing my cat
from her Technicolor
mouse dream.

Suggestions for Going Further

1. This is a *concrete*, or *visual*, poem because it looks like a river is running between the syllables. Use the poem to explain the rules for breaking words at syllables:

   Break between two consonants: in • to
   Break after a vowel if there is one consonant: tee • tering
   Break after or before prefixes, suffixes and word endings:
       fall • ing
   If a consonant has been doubled to add an ending, break
       between the consonants: step • ping

2. Students can try writing a similar poem with words broken into syllables. Possible poem ideas:

       a dog digging under a fence to escape
       stepping across a puddle
       two children digging a tunnel under the sand

   One option is to have students fold a paper twice so that there is a gap in the middle and write the words on either side of the gap.

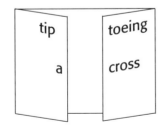

For poetry activities about concrete poems, see *The Secret Life of Words* by Betsy Franco and Maria Damon (Teaching Resource Center, 2000).

tip toeing

a cross the

ri ver

step ping

on rocks

tee tering

fall ing

in to

deli ciously

fresh cold

water

Suggestions for Going Further

1. Have students notice all the word endings in the poem. They will find the following plurals and verb endings:

Plurals
pansy - pansies
lily - lilies
howl - howls
hiss - hisses
kick - kicks
bite - bites
scratch - scratches

Verb Endings
kick - kicking
roll - rolling

2. Make the comics page of a newspaper available to students as a model. Have students draw a cartoon rendition of the poem, with the cats making sounds in speech balloons.

For poetry activities in which students learn about arrangements of words on the page, see *The Secret Life of Words* by Betsy Franco and Maria Damon (Teaching Resource Center, 2000).

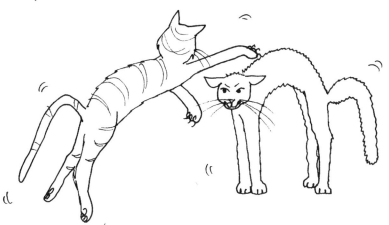

cat fight

gray fur in the pansies
black fur in the lilies
kicking and rolling
on the lawn
with howls hisses
kicks bites scratches
fur   fur   fur
flying everywhere
until the hose spray
puts a stop to it all

Suggestions for Going Further

1. Let students talk about the unusual rhyme in this poem and where it came from. (If the plural of *tooth* is *teeth*, then logically speaking, the plural of *booth* would be *beeth!*)
2. Build on the error in the poem by talking about irregular plurals in English and how they don't follow a logical pattern. Have students make a chart of the plurals for the words below, and more.

Sometimes the spelling of the word changes. Sometimes it doesn't.

tooth	teeth	mouse	mice	wolf	wolves
booth	booths	house	houses	roof	roofs
goose	geese	child	children		
moose	moose	woman	women		

Sometimes the y is changed to i and es is added. If there is a vowel before the y, just s is added.

berry	berries
monkey	monkeys

If the word ends in x, sh, ss, or ch, es is added.

box	boxes
bush	bushes
class	classes
branch	branches

Unusual Habits and Unusual Rhymes

Whenever my brother loses a tooth,

he gives it a label and stores it away.

He saves all the molars, incisors and such

in a custom-made box of baby teeth!

Whenever he goes to the shopping mall,

he wanders from telephone booth to booth,

checking for quarters, nickels, and dimes

that people have left in the telephone beeth!

poem strips start on page 97

Suggestions for Going Further

1. Brainstorm a list of collective nouns together. Ruth Heller's *A Cache of Jewels* (Grossett & Dunlap, 1987) will start the wheels turning. Some common ones are *a swarm of bees, a bed of clams, an army of ants, a school of fish, a bunch of bananas, a pod of peas, a head of hair.*
2. Talk about the unusual collective nouns in the poem and add these to the list: *a string of ponies, a watch of nightingales, a cloud of gnats, a gang of elks, a mob of kangaroos, a rafter of turkeys, a leap of leopards.* Have students draw a picture of one of the collective nouns. For fun, they could draw a literal picture, such as a string made of ponies.

A Pack of Wolves

A pack of wolves,
a hush of hares,
a tribe of goats,
a pod of seals,
a cry of hounds,
a sloth of bears,
a gam of whales,
a knot of toads—
collective nouns
we all should know.

poem strips start on page 98

Suggestions for Going Further

1. Capitalization is the grammar focus of this poem. There are proper nouns throughout, from people's names to street names to months of the year. There is even a brand name. To cement students' understanding, have them substitute other words for the capitalized words in the poem, perhaps making it humorous. For example, the people could become famous book characters.

2. Let students find three examples of possessive nouns and what they have or own in the poem (*Mrs. Lowry's honeysuckle bush, Pete's ice-cream truck,* and *Mr. Garcia's sprinkler water*). To make sure older students can differentiate between possessives and contractions, have them use each of the people in a new sentence containing a contraction. Here are some examples:

   > Mrs. Lowry's cutting her honeysuckle bush.
   > Pete's coming down the street in his truck.
   > Mr. Garcia's watering his lawn.

3. All five senses are addressed in the poem. Have students point out where this occurs. (You hear the whack of the ball, you smell the honeysuckle, you lick a popsicle, you feel the tingling on your skin, and you see the whole scene on Ramona Street.)

Ramona Street in July

You can hear the whack
of a Wilson tennis ball against the bat.
You can smell Mrs. Lowry's
honeysuckle bush.
You can lick an ice cold popsicle
from Pete's ice-cream truck.
You can feel Mr. Garcia's sprinkler water
tingling on your hot skin.
There's no place I'd rather be
than Ramona Street in July.

poem strips start on page 100

Suggestions for Going Further

1. Have students highlight the abbreviations on their copies of the student poem. Then do the same on the Desktop Pocket Chart. Make a web of abbreviations.

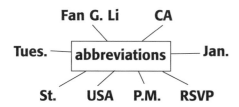

2. Ask students to analyze the form and context of the invitation. What did Fan leave out? (her telephone number) Have students write an invitation to a fantasy birthday party of their own.

You're Invited

I'm having a birthday party
   Tues., Jan. 14
   5252 Green St.
   Rome, CA 94301 USA
Be here at 3:00 P.M. on the dot for
bowling and a sleepless sleepover!
My grandmother from China says I'll be 10,
and my birth certificate says I'll be 9.
Take your pick. Please RSVP.

                    Fan G. Li

Note: *Li* is pronounced "Lee".

poem strips start on page 101

Suggestions for Going Further

1. Point out that this poem is a list of instructions preceded by a colon. The items in the list are whole sentences. Let students number the instructions on their student poems.
2. The apostrophe plays a role in this poem. It appears in contractions (*there're, you'll, that's*) and in possessives (*witch's brew, pumpkin's face*). Talk about these two uses of the apostrophe separately, and have students explain the difference. For example, students might note that a contraction stands for two separate words. (*You'll* stands for *you will*.) A possessive noun with an apostrophe means the noun has or owns something (*witch's brew*).
3. Many words in the poem rhyme. You can cover them with sticky notes on the Desktop Pocket Chart version of the poem and have students guess them. Students can also group the rhyming words into word chains and add words to each chain as shown below. They can also start chains of words which aren't in the poem but have the *oo* sound. Students can categorize them by different spelling patterns of the *oo* sound.

> do goo boo too zoo cuckoo ah-choo
> stew brew flew dew blew drew
> blue clue due hue true
> flu gnu kung fu tutu

44

Haunted House Instructions

To make a proper haunted house,
there're things you have to do:
Go get some grapes, then peel the skin,
and make an eyeball stew.

Then fill a bowl with white dry ice
to make your witch's brew.
Put on a wig and pointed hat,
and practice saying, "Boo."

Try hanging ghosts and skeletons,
and splash on ketchup goo.
Be sure to leave some time to carve
a pumpkin's face, or two.

Turn off the lights in all the rooms.
You'll need some music, too.
Invite a bunch of neighbor kids.
That's all you need to do!

Note: You can display two verses at time.

poem strips start on page 103

Suggestions for Going Further

1. This poem has a list of items preceded by a colon. Talk about words that often come before a list, such as:

   The jobs I would like are *listed below*:
   The jobs I would like are as *follows*:
   I would like *the following* jobs:

2. Here is a perfect opportunity for students to revise the poem to make it more personal. Let them rewrite the lists in the poem according to their own tastes. Use the Desktop Pocket Chart to display some of the students' versions. Be sure to tell students that their lists *don't* have to rhyme.

45

How I Feel About Jobs

The jobs I don't like
are listed below:
dog catching, tree trimming,
and taming a boa.
The jobs I would like
are listed here, too:
food tasting, band playing,
and teaching kung fu.
So that's how I feel.
Now how about you?

Suggestions for Going Further

1. Ask students to find the pairs of synonyms (and related words) in the poem. Underline or highlight them in different colors on the Desktop Pocket Chart (e.g., *home* and *house* could be yellow). Note that the synonyms are nouns, verbs, and adjectives:

   house - home
   aged - old
   tree - oak
   wind - breeze
   shimmy - shake
   tune - melody

2. Draw a number of webs on large sheets of paper and place them around the room. In the middle of each web, write a word that has many synonyms, such as *yell, beautiful, cranky, happy,* and *see.* Let students walk around and complete the webs. They can use the thesaurus as an aid.

Our Tree House

Our tree house is our secret home
way up in the aged oak.
We're like birds in a nest without any eggs.
When the wind blows hard
(not just a breeze),
we can feel the walls shimmy and shake.
In the rain, we hear a ping-pang tune,
a soft melody on the roof,
while we tell secrets and crack jokes
in our tree house way up in the old oak.

poem strips start on page 106

Suggestions for Going Further

1. Remind students that *antonyms* are words that are opposite in meaning. Point out that antonyms are the basis of
this poem. Have students find all the pairs and identify
which parts of speech they are.

hot	cold	*adjective*
black	white	*adjective*
up	down	*adverb*
weak	strong	*adjective*

2. Work with students to brainstorm a fresh list of antonyms.
Try to include nouns, verbs, adjectives, and adverbs.

hero	villain	*noun*
nighttime	daytime	*noun*
love	hate	*verb*
boil	freeze	*verb*
dull	exciting	*adjective*
quiet	talkative	*adjective*
always	never	*adverb*
nervously	calmly	*adverb*

Spider in the Tub

I turn on the tub faucets,
hot water and a little cold.
A black spider struggles
in the white porcelain,
trying to skitter up
but slipping down.
The spider's weak,
and the water's strong.
But it climbs to safety
on my paper ladder. Yikes!

poem strips start on page 107

Suggestions for Going Further

1. Remind students that *homonyms* are words that sound the same but are spelled differently and have different meanings. Students will have fun finding the words in the poem that have a homonym "partner."

   one - won
   hear - here
   there - they're - their
   heard - herd
   bear - bare
   its - it's
   weak - week
   deer - dear

2. Keep a running list of homonyms in the classroom. Possibilities include

   to - too - two   Rome - roam
   knew - new   shown - shone
   write - right   we've - weave
   lead - led   rows - rose
   passed - past   knight - night
   who's - whose   hay - hey
   dye - die

3. Give students a chance to make journal entries about situations in which they were surprised or scared. Challenge them to include at least one homonym.

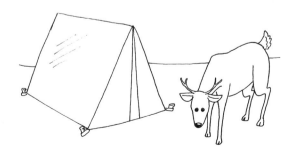

The Morning Visitor

One morning I awoke inside my tent.

I could hear a sniffling sound out there.

It came so close, I heard its breath.

I was deathly afraid there was a bear!

It stuck its head inside my tent.

My heart grew weak it was so near.

But then I smiled and laughed within.

That horrible creature was a deer!

poem strips start on page 109

Suggestions for Going Further

1. Talk about *onomatopoeia* (when words sound like what they mean), and underline or highlight the onomatopoetic words in the poem. Possibilities are *ka-boom, slamming, swishing, skipping, rrrings, scuffle,* and *shuffle*. Highlight the words on the Desktop Pocket Chart as well. Then read the poem together, emphasizing the highlighted words.
2. Brainstorm other "sound words" with the students. Here are some examples: *mumble, snort, thump, whimper, chirp, crackle, bark, giggle, roar.*
3. Ask students to describe a scene using onomatopoeia (e.g., a night scene in the country or the city, a sporting event, a rainstorm).

Sounds Before School

Ka-boom, ka-boom, a bouncing ball
slamming up against the wall,
Low notes from a clarinet,
Orange ball swishing
through the net.

Ty and Bobby calling Hope,
The sound of someone skipping rope.
First bell rrrings.
Doors open wide.
We scuffle our feet and shuffle inside.

from *Community Poems*, Scholastic, 2000

poem strips are on page 110

Suggestions for Going Further

1. The rhyming words in the poem can be used to create chains, or families, of words. Students can add to each word chain as shown below, using rhyming words or related words:
   braces spaces faces places vases mace ace tracing
   right might mighty light lightning fright frightful
   bite quite kite excite unite United States
   flaky achy take shake shaky shaken awaken
2. The poem has both *end rhymes* and *internal rhymes*. Explain to students that internal rhyme occurs when a word in the middle of a line rhymes with another word in the poem. Have students find the internal rhyme (*bite's* rhymes with *night, right,* and *sight*).

For poetry activities using chains of words, end rhyme, internal rhyme, and off-rhyme, see *The Secret Life of Words,* by Betsy Franco and Maria Damon (Teaching Resource Center, 2000).

Braces

I have to have braces
to close up the spaces
and headgear at night,
since my bite's not quite right.
They make me look flaky.
My teeth feel achy.
But when they're all straight,
it'll be "out of sight!"

poem strips start on page 111

Suggestions for Going Further

1. Let students find all the mistakes in the poem and correct them:
   Capitalize names like <u>John</u>,
   and don't let sentences run on and on.
   Don't mix up words if <u>their</u>
   sounds are the same.
   They mean different things—
   <u>it's</u> just like a game.
   And just <u>because</u> it's *sing* and *sang* and *sung,*
   doesn't mean it's *think,* and *thank,* and *thunk*!

2. Elaborate on each grammar element that was misused in the poem:
   capitalization
   run-on sentences*
   homonyms
   slang
   conjugating irregular verbs
   *Lines 1, 2 and 3 in the poem are not a run-on sentence, but rather a sentence that has a few unnecessary words. (Run-ons are sentences in which too many independent clauses are combined.)

3. Do students have other mistakes to add to the list? Let them write a sentence that breaks a grammar, spelling or punctuation rule. Show their sentences on the overhead and have the class correct them. Examples:
   Make sure the subject and verb agrees when you write.
   (*agree*)
   Be carefull to look up words you don't know how to spell.
   (*careful*)
   The teacher always says, Use quotation marks correctly."
   (*"Use . . .*)

Grammar Rules

Capitalize names like john,

and don't let sentences run on

and on and on.

Don't mix up words if there

sounds are the same.

They mean different things—

its just like a game.

And just cuz it's *sing* and *sang* and *sung,*

doesn't mean it's *think,* and *thank,* and *thunk!*

Poem Strip Contents

"What Goes Around" 53
Turning Down the Heat 54
My Best Friend and I 55
Sharing a Room 57
New Kid 59
Birthday Money 60
My Moods 62
Timothy Jones and His Yo-Yo 63
Everyone's Family 64
The Package That's Me 66
Habitats 67
Dear Thomas Alva Edison 68
The Predator's Bad Day 70
My Favorite Music 71
Math Poems 73
a bare foot 74
Babysitting 75
Three People and a Pizza 77
Once There Were Buffalo 78
Time Travel 80
Imagine 81

Someday 83
I run 84
You Never Know Which Seeds Will Grow 85
"Crazy Hair Day" 87
Dog on the Loose 89
If...Then 90
Moonlight 91
tip...toeing 93
cat fight 94
Unusual Habits and Unusual Rhymes 96
A Pack of Wolves 97
Ramona Street in July 98
You're Invited 100
Haunted House Instructions 101
How I Feel About Jobs 103
Our Tree House 105
Spider in the Tub 106
The Morning Visitor 107
Sounds Before School 109
Braces 110
Grammar Rules 111

Note: The page number appears on the bottom strip on each page. To avoid confusion, we recommend that you make one copy and white out the page number before copying the poetry strips onto card stock.

"What Goes Around"

I helped Bo,

Bo helped Mo,

Mo helped Mei,

Mei helped Ray,

Ray helped Bea,

and Bea helped me.

⁸ "What goes around comes around."

⁹ That's how it oughta be.

¹ Turning Down the Heat

² Ticked off

³ Angry

⁴ Furious

⁵ Boiling

⁶ That was how my feelings grew.

Breathing

deeply

Cooling

down

Now that has changed my point of view!

My Best Friend and I

Sometimes we're magnets,

drawn to each other like

a negative and a positive force.

Other days we're like two positives

(or more like two negatives)

pushing away from each other,

never able to get too close.

But then we flip around somehow

and we're inseparable again.

Sharing a Room

Sally Sue is very messy.

She leaves toys thrown everywhere.

She's got laundry on her bookshelf,

gobs of toothpaste on her chair.

As for me, I'm neat and tidy.

I have labels on each drawer.

8 Everyday I use the vacuum.

9 You could eat right off my floor.

10 We divided up the bedroom,

11 drew a line across the floor.

12 We made sure that it was even,

13 neither one was getting more.

14 She allows me in the closet,

15 and I let her use the door.

Though the plan is not quite perfect,

it's much better than before!

New Kid

Like a scarecrow,

I stand with awkward arms,

while everyone laughs and plays.

Like a yo-yo,

I move in and out

7 of the crowd of kids.

8 I guess I'll go home alone again.

9 But hey!

10 There's Joe and he's yelling,

11 "Wanna play?"

1

Birthday Money

2 My auntie gave me birthday cash,

60

and I'm wondering what to do.

I might see movies all day long

and bring a friend or two.

Oh no, I just remembered

what I really need to do.

I have to pay for the window

that my soccer ball went through!

My Moods

Timid, bold,

friendly, mad,

silly, somber,

happy, sad.

I laugh, I scowl.

I smile, I frown.

My moods are always

up and down.

Timothy Jones and His Yo-Yo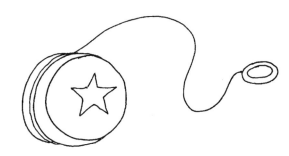

In the beginning,

I couldn't do much—

just make it unwind

and untangle the string.

6 Then Timothy taught me 'bout

7 walkin' the dog, hoppin' the fence,

8 and a lot of cool things.

9 It's quite unbelievable, let me tell you,

10 what Timothy Jones and his yo-yo can do.

1 Everyone's Family

2 Everyone's family's from someplace else

(except for American Indians).

Families came from close and far,

in peacetime and in wartime, too.

Some wore babushkas on their heads,

and some had pigtails down their backs.

Some felt upset, but most had hope

for their life in America—different and new.

The Package That's Me

206 snow-white

bones covered by more than

600 sinewy muscles nourished by

60,000 miles of pulsating blood

vessels and encased in

20 square feet of protective

skin which also houses

a heart the size of a fist

that brings it all to life.

Habitats

The lizard slithers from under the rocks.

She warms her scales in the morning sun.

The frog sets up camp on the edge of the pond.

He contemplates his afternoon meal.

6 The bat unfurls his folded wings.

7 He exits his cave to hunt by the moon.

8 I throw off the covers and crawl out of bed.

9 I toss a shirt on my bedroom floor.

10 But unlike the lizard, the frog, and the bat,

11 my mom makes me clean up my habitat!

1 June 4, 2000

2 Dear Thomas Alva Edison,

Someone invented the Internet

and someone invented the wheel.

But you're the greatest inventor,

at least that's the way I feel.

You made the electric lightbulb,

the movie camera, the phonograph.

If I'd been alive when you were alive,

I would have asked for your autograph.

Sincerely,
Jamie Taft

The Predator's Bad Day

The predator

spots its prey,

who understands

its predicament,

snaps into motion,

and disappears.

There is no connection.

There is no consumption—

a sad conclusion for the predator,

but a sensational day for the prey!

My Favorite Music

My music sounds

like the roof is being torn off.

It's blacks and reds and shocking pinks,

and it tastes like burning rubber.

"The decibels!

The frequencies!

The vibrations!

My eardrums!"

yells Mom.

"Turn *that music* down!!"

Math Poems

colors

child

wind $)\overline{\text{fall}}$

- nap

-leaves

whining

winter

squirrels in winter

thunder

x 3 months

lightning

hibernation

wind

+ rain that's warm

summer storm

a bare foot

a bumblebee

a sting

a yelp

a welt

some ache

some ice

some shoes

next time!

Babysitting

2 "Three-fifty an hour," said nice Mrs. Fine.

3 "Can you come by tomorrow from 5 to 9?"

4 "I'll just ask my mother," I said with a wave.

5 "Of course," said my mom. "They're so well-behaved.

6 I thought to myself, "Well, I like to play games,

7 but after four hours, it's not quite the same.

8 But I like both her kids and they love me to read.

9 Three-fifty times four is just what I need!"

Three People and a Pizza

The pepperoni pizza had been

cut up into fourths.

We couldn't divide it evenly,

as you can see, of course.

Then Julie cut each piece again.

She cut them into thirds.

At first her cutting seemed to make

the problem even worse.

But then she passed the pieces out—

to me and her and Steven.

Why sure enough, it all worked out,

and all our shares were even!

Once There Were Buffalo

They used the buffalo for food,

leather clothing, tipis, robes,

blankets, spoons, cups, knives,

bowstrings, and musical instruments.

Then along came the railroad,

sharpshooters like Wild Bill Cody, and more.

And after a while, there weren't

many buffalo for musical instruments,

bowstrings, knives, cups, spoons, blankets,

robes, tipis, leather clothing, or food.

Time Travel

I thought it would be fun

to come over on the Mayflower,

until I heard that the colonists ate

sheep's tongue pie, stewed eel,

creamed turkey and oysters,

and boiled pigeons.

Peanut chews, hot molasses cider, and apple pie sound good, but I think I'll pass on the Mayflower for now.

Imagine

Can you imagine being in a covered wagon and picking up buffalo chips for the night fire?

Can you imagine snakes and spiders

nestled in your nighttime blanket?

What must it be like to float across rivers

on a wagon bed

or wobble along steep mountain passes?

Someone like you was on those covered wagons.

Imagine.

Someday

There were George

and Thomas and Abe

and Franklin and John

and Richard and Bill.

Someday they'll be

Barbara and Ebony

and Sarah and Tolu

and Shoko and Aziz

and José.

11

Someday.

1 I run

2 I race

3 I leap

4 I lunge

5 I dive

84

I catch

I squeeze

I capture the ball

at the tip of my mitt.

What a feeling I get!

You Never Know Which Seeds Will Grow

When Bo was very little,

he had lots and lots of pets.

4 Right now he cares for neighbors' dogs.

5 Someday he'll be a vet.

6 Kathleen made hook shots in the sink

7 a long, long time ago.

8 Right now she is a point guard,

9 and someday she'll be a pro.

10 You never know

11 which seeds will grow!

Samantha used to put on skits

and sing with her guitar.

Right now she has the lead in plays.

Someday she'll be a star.

"Crazy Hair Day"

It was "Crazy Hair Day,"

and this is what we wore:

silly pigtails in front,

green and blue hair dye,

hair sticking out all over,

and spiked and moussed bangs.

Hey, even the guinea pig

had his hair sticking every-which-way,

but then he's always having

a crazy hair day!

Dog on the Loose

He's yippy and yappy

with a deep black coat and bold white spots.

Bring out an old, mangled tennis ball,

and he'll be all over you.

He'll shake with his softly-padded paw

if you only ask.

But watch out for his drippy, slobbery tongue.

9 Have you seen him?

10 That dog is loose again!

11 Oh yes, his name is *Houdini.*

1   If...Then

2 If I cut my toenails,

3 then the bus won't ever come on time.

4 If the sun forgets to come up this morning,

5 then my dog will definitely have fleas.

If my bike has a completely flat tire, then it won't storm on my birthday.

If my cat washes himself very carefully, then my dad will take me to miniature golf.

If I make this totally impossible hook shot, then you'll have to clean my room for me!

Moonlight

Moonlight

3 fragile and fleeting

4 tiptoed mindlessly

5 over to the window

6 and burst through,

7 filling the room with

8 a luminous glow

9 and rousing my cat

10 from her Technicolor

mouse dream.

tip   toeing

a   cross the

ri   ver

step   ping

on   rocks

tee   tering

fall   ing

8   in   to

9   deli   ciously

10   fresh   cold

11   wa   ter

1   cat fight

2   gray fur in the pansies

3   black fur in the lilies

4   kicking and rolling

on the lawn

with howls hisses

kicks bites scratches

fur fur fur
flying everywhere

until the hose spray

puts a stop to it all

Unusual Habits and Unusual Rhymes

Whenever my brother loses a tooth,

he gives it a label and stores it away.

He saves all the molars, incisors and such

in a custom-made box of baby teeth!

Whenever he goes to the shopping mall,

he wanders from telephone booth to booth,

checking for quarters, nickels, and dimes

that people have left in the telephone beeth!

A Pack of Wolves

A pack of wolves,

a hush of hares,

a tribe of goats,

a pod of seals,

a cry of hounds,

a sloth of bears,

a gam of whales,

a knot of toads—

collective nouns

we all should know.

Ramona Street in July

You can hear the whack

of a Wilson tennis ball against the bat.

You can smell Mrs. Lowry's honeysuckle bush.

You can lick an ice cold popsicle from Pete's ice-cream truck.

You can feel Mr. Garcia's sprinkler water tingling on your hot skin.

There's no place I'd rather be than Ramona Street in July.

You're Invited

1. I'm having a birthday party
2. Tues., Jan. 14
3. 5252 Green St.
4. Rome, CA 94301 USA
5. Be here at 3:00 P.M. on the dot for
6. bowling and a sleepless sleepover!
7. My grandmother from China says I'll be 10,

and my birth certificate says I'll be 9.

Take your pick. Please RSVP.

Fan G. Li

Haunted House Instructions

To make a proper haunted house,

there're things you have to do:

Go get some grapes, then peel the skin,

5 and make an eyeball stew.

6 Then fill a bowl with white dry ice

7 to make your witch's brew.

8 Put on a wig and pointed hat,

9 and practice saying, "Boo."

10 Try hanging ghosts and skeletons,

11 and splash on ketchup goo.

12 Be sure to leave some time to carve

a pumpkin's face, or two.

Turn off the lights in all the rooms.

You'll need some music, too.

Invite a bunch of neighbor kids.

That's all you need to do!

How I Feel About Jobs

The jobs I don't like

are listed below:

4 dog catching, tree trimming,

5 and taming a boa.

6 The jobs I would like

7 are listed here, too:

8 food tasting, band playing,

9 and teaching kung fu.

10 So that's how I feel.

11 Now how about you?

Our Tree House

Our tree house is our secret home

way up in the aged oak.

We're like birds in a nest without any eggs.

When the wind blows hard

(not just a breeze),

we can feel the walls shimmy and shake.

In the rain, we hear a ping-pang tune,

⁹ a soft melody on the roof,

¹⁰ while we tell secrets and crack jokes

¹¹ in our tree house way up in the old oak.

¹ Spider in the Tub

² I turn on the tub faucets,

³ hot water and a little cold.

⁴ A black spider struggles

⁵ in the white porcelain,

trying to skitter up

but slipping down.

The spider's weak,

and the water's strong.

But it climbs to safety

on my paper ladder. Yikes!

The Morning Visitor

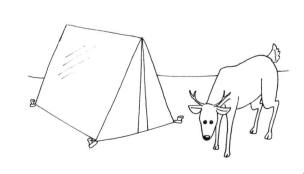

² One morning I awoke inside my tent.

³ I could hear a sniffling sound out there.

⁴ It came so close, I heard its breath.

⁵ I was deathly afraid there was a bear!

⁶ It stuck its head inside my tent.

⁷ My heart grew weak it was so near.

⁸ But then I smiled and laughed within.

⁹ That horrible creature was a deer!

Sounds Before School

Ka-boom, ka-boom, a bouncing ball

slamming up against the wall,

Low notes from a clarinet,

Orange ball swishing

through the net.

Ty and Bobby calling Hope,

The sound of someone skipping rope.

First bell rrrings.

Doors open wide.

We scuffle our feet and shuffle inside.

1

Braces

2 I have to have braces

3 to close up the spaces

4 and headgear at night,

5 since my bite's not quite right.

6 They make me look flaky.

7 My teeth feel achy.

8 But when they're all straight,

9 it'll be "out of sight!"

1 Grammar Rules

2 Capitalize names like john,

3 and don't let sentences run on

4 and on and on.

5 Don't mix up words if there

6 sounds are the same.

7 They mean different things—

8 its just like a game.

9 And just cuz it's *sing* and *sang* and *sung*,

10 doesn't mean it's *think*, and *thank*, and *thunk!*